FIRST FRUITS
SEED OFFERING

BY

DR. RONALD E. COTTLE

All Scripture quotations are from the King James Version or New King James Version unless otherwise noted.

Copyright © 2006
Ronald E. Cottle

World rights reserved. No part of this publication may be stored in a retrieval system, transmitted, or reproduced in any way, including but not limited to photocopy, photograph, magnetic or other record, without prior agreement and written permission of the author.

FOREWARD

Welcome to this special gift edition of the book, *First Fruits Seed Offering*, written by Dr. Ron Cottle. As a spiritual son to Dr. Cottle, I have practiced the first fruits lifestyle and have enjoyed "another dimension of God" as he says.

We are releasing this 2021 gift edition in response to the current conditions in the Church brought about by the Covid-19 pandemic. First published in 2006 by Dr. Cottle, now, more than ever, God's plan for financing the Kingdom is needed. We believe that the first fruits seed offering is the missing ingredient.

Our prayer is that you will sow your first fruits seed offering and experience God's benefit package that automatically comes forth!

> *And he (Jesus) said, "The kingdom of God is like this: like a man scatters seed on the ground. And he sleeps and gets up, night and day, and the seed sprouts and grows—he does not know how.* ***By itself*** *(Greek* ***autómatos****— automatically, of its own accord) the soil produces a crop: first the grass, then the head of grain, then the full grain in the head. But when the crop permits, he sends in the sickle right away, because the harvest has come"* (***Mark 4:26–29:*** *Lexham English Bible) (Emphasis mine).*

Dr. Thomas Hale, Multiplier, Ron Cottle Ministries
January 2021

TABLE OF CONTENTS

INTRODUCTION

AN OPPORTUNITY TO EXPERIENCE BREAKTHROUGH

I have a profound interest in the lands of the Bible: comparing how they are today with how they were in the days of the early church. I usually travel overseas every November either to Israel or to Greece to walk in the footsteps of Jesus in Israel or follow the paths of Paul in Greece. With the twenty-five or so people I generally take with me on these discovery trips, we traverse those roads and discover, "This happened here," and, "There is where that occurred." The Bible is both our guide and textbook for this powerful and often emotional journey. We have a wonderful time studying and learning about God's awesome acts in history portrayed in Scripture.

Now, my goal as you read these pages is to have you journey with me; so, have your textbook, the Bible, and a journal in front of you. We will begin our exploration in Exodus 23 then travel through many other books of the Bible to reach our final destination for this trip. I am confident that what you will find is very relevant to you today. As your personal guide, I am going to lead you through and help you to discover the profound truths concerning the **First Fruits Seed Offering.**

Fulfill God's purposes in your life. What I'm sharing with you literally rocked me to my shoe leather. You will share in my amazement as you see how this eternal truth and spiritual principle is woven through every page of the Bible. You will also discover how to implement the First Fruits Seed Offering so that you may implement it to fulfill the eternal purposes of God for your life.

Experience breakthrough. I am offering you an opportunity to experience breakthrough, to move into another dimension in God. You will need to bring more than your Bible with you, though. To participate in all that is available to you, you must have a deep desire to achieve that higher level. You must be willing to work with me as we progress through this journey. Together we will embark on an exciting expedition through the Bible that will speak to your spirit a *rhema,* a revelation word, that will directly impact every facet of your life.

Get ready for God's *rhema* word! I believe with every bone in my body that this *rhema* word is for the Church, the Body of Christ, and it's for this particular hour. So, gather your tools, prepare you heart and mind to receive fresh manna from God, and keep your journal handy. Are you ready?

Ronald E. Cottle, Ph.D., Ed.D.
Beacon University
Spring, 2006

CHAPTER 1

AND GOD SPOKE ALL THESE WORDS...

Three times thou shalt keep a feast unto me in the year. Thou shalt keep the feast of unleavened bread: (thou shalt eat unleavened bread seven days, as I commanded thee, in the time appointed of the month Abib; for in it thou camest out from Egypt: and none shall appear before me empty:) . . . The first of the firsffruits of thy land thou shalt bring into the house of the LORD thy God.

Exodus 23:14,15,19a

The Three Feasts

Our journey begins by studying some of the history surrounding the Jewish calendar and the three feasts God commanded Moses to celebrate annually. Then we will move on to explore the seven points, the seven blessings, of participating in the **First Fruits Seed Offering.** We are heading toward a breakthrough that God has designed for us to discover as we earnestly seek it in His Word.

The Jewish calendar or year is built around three feasts. We need to understand that our Biblical timeline, the blessing timeline, is built around these same three feasts. To uncover the principles of the **First Fruits Seed Offering,** we need to return to the moment when God gave Moses the original calendar. We must enter into the time of the Great Exodus from Egypt.

The children of Israel left Egypt and were delivered by God into to the Desert of Sinai. They journeyed to the base of Mount Sinai. The Bible records that their journey to Sinai took three months. They pitched their tents there at the base of Mt. Sinai and then the Lord called Moses to come up and meet with Him. This exchange between God and Moses starts in Exodus 19. After following some initial instructions from God, Moses received the Ten Commandments and then the directions for how to prosper in the Promised Land. Realize that the children of Israel had been slaves for so long that they no longer knew how to survive on their own.

Exodus 20 begins, **"And God spoke all these words."** It was important that the people understood that God was the One giving them these instructions. Moses was to convey to the children of Israel all that God was commanding them to do, not as a slave master but as a loving Lord. As you study these chapters, you will discover that Moses made several trips up and down the mountain. Exodus 23:13 reads, "Be careful to do everything I have said to you" (NIV). God was serious about His people being obedient to His very specific and detailed instructions.

Now, in Exodus 23:14-17, God reveals His timeline for the Three Annual Feasts. We will take them one by one to gain a basic understanding of God's purpose in His calendar for these offerings.

> *Three times thou shalt keep a feast unto me in the* ***year.*** *Thou shall keep the **feast of unleavened bread.** Thou shalt eat unleavened bread seven*

*days as **I** commanded in the time appointed in the month Aviv; for in it you came out of Egypt. And none shall appear before me empty.*

*And the **feast of harvest,** the firsffruits of thy labours, which thou hast sown in the field: and the **feast of ingathering,** which is in the end of the year, when thou hast gathered in thy labours out of the field. **Three** times in the **year** all thy males shall appear before the Lord **GOD** (emphasis added).*

Passover—The Feast of Unleavened Bread—First Fruits

*Thou shall keep the **feast of unleavened bread.** Thou shalt eat unleavened bread seven days as **I** commanded in the time appointed in the month Aviv; for in it you came out of Egypt. And none shall appear before me empty.*

Exodus 23:15

The Feast of Unleavened Bread is the first festival that God commanded Moses to initiate with His people. At times, the Passover is spoken of as the Feast of Unleavened Bread. Now, when the Bible mentions Passover, it is referring to the entire eight-day feast. *Pescah,* Passover, starts at six o'clock on Friday night and goes through the next day until six o'clock Saturday night. That's the actual Day of Passover. Then Passover Sunday begins the Feast of Unleavened Bread which lasts for the next seven days, during which they could not eat or cook with leaven (yeast). We need to travel back to Exodus 12 to read the story of the first Passover and the first time the Feast of Unleavened Bread is mentioned in the Bible.

*And ye shall observe the **feast of unleavened bread;** for in this selfsame day have I brought your armies out of the land of Egypt: therefore shall ye observe this day in your generations by an ordinance for ever.*

Exodus 12:17

*And it shall come to pass, when your children shall say unto you, What mean ye by this service? That ye shall say, It is the sacrifice of the **LORD'S** passover, who passed over the houses of the children of Israel in Egypt, when he smote the Egyptians, and delivered our houses. And the people bowed the head and worshipped.*

Exodus 12:26-27, emphasis added

God wanted Israel not only to celebrate this feast but also to intentionally explain to the next generation why they were celebrating the Passover. God wanted them to follow His instructions and to know the reason behind the feast.

The Feast of Unleavened Bread ends on the Sunday following the second Sabbath Saturday. That Sunday is called First Fruits, the time to bring the seed offering unto God. Now, this is the way every good, godly Hebrew was to begin his year.

1. He worked the first month to get the seed.

2. Then in the second month the giving Hebrew brought that seed as an offering to sow as an item of faith to God.

3. His act of giving in faith signified that God was to be his partner, and that everything he had belonged to God.

4. By giving, the giver proclaimed his confident
   expectation and hope that God would bring to him
   the harvest for the upcoming year.

The Feast of Harvest—The Feast of Weeks—Pentecost

*And the **feast of harvest,** the firsffruits of thy
labours, which thou hast sown in the field.*
Exodus 23:16a

The second feast arrives fifty days after Passover. In the Old
Testament, it is further explained in Leviticus 23:15-16 and
Deuteronomy 16:9-12. In the New Testament it is called
Pentecost and occurred ten days after Jesus' Ascension. The
Holy Spirit was outpoured on the Day of Pentecost (see
Acts 2:1-4).

**The Day of Atonement—The Feast of Ingathering—
The Feast of Tabernacles**

*...and the **feast of ingathering,** which is in the end
of the year when thou hast gathered in thy labours
out of the field.*
Exodus 23:16b

The third feast of the year is the Day of Atonement to be
celebrated on the tenth day of the seventh month, Kishri in the
Hebrew calendar.

*And the **LORD** spake unto Moses, saying, "Also on
the tenth day of this seventh month there shall be a
day of atonement: it shall be an holy convo-
cation unto you; and ye shall afflict your souls,*

and offer an offering made by fire unto the
LORD."

Leviticus 23:26-27

On the fifteenth day of the seventh month the Feast   of Tabernacles begins.

> *And the **LORD** spake unto Moses, saying, "Speak unto the children of Israel, saying, The fifteenth day of this seventh month shall be the feast of tabernacles for seven days unto the **LORD**. On the first day shall be an holy convocation: ye shall do no servile work therein. Seven days ye shall offer an offering made by fire unto the **LORD**: on the eighth day shall be an holy convocation unto you; and ye shall offer an offering made by fire unto the **LORD**: it is a solemn assembly; and ye shall do no servile work therein."*

Leviticus 23:33-36. See also verses 39-43

Now, this is God's calendar, His timeline of blessing. We are also on this timeline whether we recognize it or not. Let's quickly review what we just learned.

- The New Year begins. We work one month.

- Then we celebrate the **Passover-6 P.M.** Friday through 6 P.M. on Saturday.

- That Sunday begins the *Feast of Unleavened Bread,* lasting seven days.

- The Sunday following the second Sabbath is **First Fruits Seed Offering.**

- Fifty days later we celebrate the second feast—The ***Feast of the*** Harvest—Pentecost

12

- The third feast begins on the tenth day of the seventh month—the **Day of Atonement.** Then on the fifteenth day of the tenth month we begin the *Feast of Tabernacles,* also known as the Feast of the Ingathering that lasts seven days.

The Calendar

Indeed, we don't recognize this blessing timeline in the biblical calendar because in A.D. 325, at the Council of Nicea, the emperor Constantine decided that the Julian calendar was to be used instead of the Jewish calendar. That changed the year from a lunar calendar to a solar calendar. The Julian calendar, originated by Julius Caesar back in 47 B.C., was later modified even more by Pope Gregory XIII in 1582. Today we use this Gregorian calendar.

The consequence of all this is that we have lost sight of God's blessing timeline. The **First Fruits Seed Offering** was to be given at Passover, bringing about the outpouring of His Spirit, leading to atonement and reconciliation to God. The cycle was to repeat again for the coming year and flow on from generation to generation. God's timeline, His design to bring about His blessings to His people, is no longer apparent today as we follow the Gregorian calendar.

Passover, the Feast of Unleavened Bread and First Fruits Sunday

Now, **I** need to clarify a few things before we plunge into the seven great blessings that come from the **First Fruits Seed Offering.** First, Passover, the Feast of Unleavened Bread, and First Fruits Sunday are all really one feast. Remember that God commanded Moses to celebrate three feasts a year. This eight-day festival, which includes

Passover, then the Feast of Unleavened Bread followed by First Fruits Sunday, is considered one of those three feasts. Therefore, when the Bible talks about Passover, it is also referring to the Feast of Unleavened Bread and First Fruits Sunday. No matter which one is mentioned in Scripture, it is talking about the same eight-day festival. It is important to understand that.

Three Ways to Give to God

I am going to show you the seven blessings released by the First Fruits offering. But the second point I must clarify is that this First Fruits offering is not the regular tithe. Many people are confused about the fact that these are not the same. Furthermore, the **First Fruits Seed Offering** is not the offering we give above the tithe.

Let me briefly explain a few insights about each one of the three ways to give to God in addition to the giving of alms.

1) The Tithe. The tithe is the debt owed. Nobody *gives* the tithe; we pay a tithe because tithing preceded the law, it's not legalism. It was around long before Moses' Law, so don't ever call a tither a legalist. He is not a legalist. He is far deeper into God than the legalism of even the Law of Moses.

Tithing was practiced even before Abraham. It was second nature to him because it was a vital part of his way of life. Tithing began at creation, going all the way back to Genesis 1:11. This basic principle of seedtime and harvest, tithing, is in the very fabric of the earth's core.

Every person, not just Christians and Jews, owes the tithe. Tithes are rent on God's property. Why do I say that? We are all breathing God's air; we are all living on God's ground;

14

we have each built a place on God's property;therefore, we all owe rent. We need to be clear on this. Read Psalm 24:1 and 1 Corinthians 10:26. They both tell us: "The earth *is* the LORD'S, and all its fullness, the world and those who dwell therein" (NKJV).

Therefore, the tithe is the rent, and everybody who doesn't pay it has a curse upon his life.

> *Will a man rob God? Yet ye have robbed me. But ye say, Wherein have we robbed thee? In tithes **and** offerings. Ye are cursed with a curse: for ye have robbed me, even this whole nation. Bring ye all the tithes into the storehouse, that there may be meat in mine house, and prove me now herewith, saith the LORD of hosts, if I will not open you the windows of heaven, and pour you out a blessing, that there shall not be room enough to receive it.*
>
> Malachi 3:8-10, **emphasis** added

2) Offerings. Now, what about the offerings also mentioned in the Malachi 3:8? Note the word "and" in this verse. These offerings are a gift to God on top of or in addition to the required tithe. Malachi 3:9 tells us that withholding either the tithe or the offering is robbing God. But one cannot give an offering until he has paid his tithe. Offerings are given above the tithe which then allows God to open the windows of heaven and pour out His blessings. He promises so much of a blessing that there shall not be room enough to receive or contain it. Offerings that can produce returns of thirty, sixty and a hundred fold, if they are sowed in tithed ground.

> *But this I say, He which soweth sparingly shall reap also sparingly; and he which soweth boun-*

tifully shall reap also bountifully. Every man according as he purposeth in his heart, so let him give; not grudgingly, or of necessity: for God loveth a cheerful giver. And God is able to make all grace abound toward you; that ye,
always having all sufficiency in all things, may abound to every good work.

2 Corinthians 9:6-8

3) First Fruits Seed Offering. Now then, what about the third way to give to God? That's the First Fruits seed offering. We are going to study this in depth, but basically this First Fruits covenant seed offering is given once a year, ideally on the fourteenth of the month Aviv, which is roughly April the twenty-fourth. This is a one-time-a-year seed gift that we are to sow to God. As the Body of Christ, we have been a little delinquent with our First Fruits offerings, and we have missed a bunch of blessings as a result. We need to get caught up as this is the way to achieve breakthrough within God's timeline.

We are still called, as His people, to participate in giving a First Fruits Seed Offering. As we do, we individually acknowledge that God is the owner of everything in our lives. This once-a-year offering further indicates that we understand we are each functioning as God's partner here on the earth.

Why is this offering so important for us to comprehend? As a member of the Body of Christ, you need to realize and declare that in your body you are now God's instrument. This means is that you have come to understand it's not up to a doctor to keep you well and healthy. Your Life Partner, God in Christ Jesus, has taken over full responsibility. It's up to your Life Partner to keep you in good functioning condition so that together you again accomplish His purposes for your life.

In this offering you are stating that God is your Partner in everything that touches your life. You are acknowledging that your finances and your bank account belong to Him. God's Word says He promises you a profit, a multiplication of your seed—not a loss.

> *Now he that ministereth seed to the sower both minister bread for your food, and multiply your seed sown, and increase the fruits of your righteousness.*
>
> 2 Corinthians 9:10

Now return to where we started in Exodus 23. Look again at verses 14 and 15:

> *Three times **thou shalt keep** a feast unto me in the year. **Thou shall keep** the feast of unleavened bread. **Thou shalt** eat unleavened bread seven days as I **commanded** in the time appointed in the month Aviv; for in it you came out of Egypt. And none shall appear before me empty.*

When God says, "Thou shalt," it indicates that this is not optional. It is a direct command of God. But, in most cases, we find we have not been obeying these instructions.

Implement God's Timeline of Blessing!

It's time we started! We are going to learn how because we now know it's not an option.

We can get on God's calendar and implement the blessing timeline of Scripture, but we are going to have to do certain things to accomplish this change of lifestyle. It is going to take some work, some rethinking of "how we have always done things." Wouldn't you really prefer to be on God's timeline January through December rather than on the man-made Gregorian calendar? Can you see now that the Gregorian calendar is another deception of the enemy to keep us from the blessings of God?

Let's begin by learning how to celebrate the First Fruits offering. Our original text, Exodus 23:15, says:

> *...and **none** shall appear before Me empty.*

It says **none** are to come without an offering. We **all** are to come with a gift in hand at the beginning of the year—our spiritual year. With it, we are **each** say to God, "This is my seed on the basis of which **I** expect that You will bless me this year."

Our obedience to this one command begins an incredible process that the church has lost because of Constantine and the switch to the Gregorian calendar. We have lost it due to what the world has chosen as our "year," but **I** want to show you we can regain it. By studying God's original instruc-tions to Moses, learning about the First Fruits offering, I believe that we will come into a new dimension—a new place in God.

Journey with me now as we study, discover, uncover and then implement God's timeline for the First Fruits Seed Offering. Let's discover all that we can about the First **Fruits Seed Offering** and the *Seven Results* God promises as we follow His calendar instead of man's timeline.

CHAPTER 2

YOUR WATCHMAN, SENTINEL AND GUIDE

"Behold, I send an Angel before thee, to keep thee in the way, and to bring thee into the place which I have prepared."

Exodus 23:20

It's my desire that you learn to discern for yourself what I consider the single most important time of the year in the Spirit. By revealing each of the seven results available through participation in the *First Fruits Seed Offering,* I believe that you will not only come to share in my conclusion but desire to become an active participant as well.

Though there were three feasts given to Moses by God, understanding the significance of the first one, the Feast of Unleavened Bread, is the key to uncovering these seven life-changing benefits. Recognizing the full impact of this festival which culminates with a First Fruits Sunday celebration is pivotal to attaining a breakthrough in your life.

All seven of the blessings that attend the *First Fruits Seed Offering* are listed in Exodus 23. We will travel from here through the Scriptures to discover how God carried out these blessings in the lives of others and to uncover what effect this offering had on each one's fulfilling his or her God-given future.

The first resulting blessing is revealed in Exodus 23:20:

> *"Behold, **I** send an Angel before you to keep you in the way and to bring you into the place which **I** have prepared."*

To uncover the depth of each blessing, you must carefully read what each verse is saying to you. Do you see the multiple **promises** described in Exodus 23:20?

First of all, consider the word *Angel.* God says, "Bring the First Fruits seed, sow the seed, and I will release the Angel." You release the precious seed and God will release the power. Also note that the word *Angel* is correctly capitalized in this verse. In the Old Testament, a capitalized *Angel* refers to the pre-incarnate Christ Himself. (Note: Gen. 3:24; Ex. 4:16; Josh. 5:13-14; Ps. 18:11; 104:4; Isa. 61:2; Mal. 2:7). In this verse the article should be rendered "the Angel."

The Angel Will Do Two Things

This first result is essential in uncovering this blessing pattern. God says, "Sow the seed, and **I** will release to you the Angel." The Angel that God releases will do two things for those who are willing to obey. Look again at Exodus 23:20 to see why this is so vital to in being able to fulfill your personal destiny:

> *"Behold, **I** send an Angel before you to **keep you in the way** and to **bring you into the place which I have prepared"** (emphasis added).*

The Angel will "keep you in the way." Now, the word *way* here is *derek* in Hebrew and it means "path." So, the Angel will keep you in the path.

We also need to look at the Hebrew word for *keep,* which is *shamar.* It actually has three meanings. The first meaning is *watchman.* When we sow the First Fruits seed, the Bible says that the Angel will come and be a watchman on the walls of our lives. He will see everything that's coming and going. We will be under his watchful eyes.

The second meaning of the word *shamar* is "a guard, or a *sentinel."* Picture a soldier who walks around us and protects us from the invasion of the enemy into our lives.

The third meaning of *shamar* is "a *guide."* So, we have a watchman, a sentinel, and now a guide. But this Angel is more than just a guide; He is a shepherd who leads us into the proper place.

Can you begin to picture what this means to you personally? This is just the first result of sowing a First Fruits seed; immediately you have the Angel, sent by God to watch over, guard and guide you. That means your affairs will become His affairs. Your problems will become His problems. Your opportunities will be seen by His watchful eye, and He will carefully guide you into the proper ones like a good shepherd.

Your affairs will be His affairs!
Your problems will be His problems!

That leads us to the second thing the Bible says the Angel released by God is to do for those who sow the First Fruits seed. This Angel has quite an impressive job description!

> *"and to **bring you into the place which I have prepared"***

The Angel will not only keep you safely on the designated path, but will bring you into the place the Father has prepared just for you. By examining this verse more closely, you will discover two important aspects of this blessing that could easily be overlooked at first glance. Number one is that God has prepared a particular place specifically designed for you.

To determine how crucial this detail is to experiencing breakthrough, we need to understand what the word *place* means. As we look at the Greek word for place, *topos,* we think of the English word *topography* which leads us to geography and the belief that God has a geographical place where we will be blessed in life more than any other. That is a true assumption but it's only part of what *topos* really means to a child of God.

The English word *topic* also comes from *topos* leading us to the concept of personal *destiny.* God has a unique destiny already mapped out expressly for you. By God's design, a special anointing is available to you to fulfill your calling and accomplish His purpose for you here on the earth. God has known from before the foundations of the world precisely why He made you as well as the path you're to follow to arrive at that precise place He has prepared for you (see Eph. 2:10 and Jer. 1:5).

Your First Fruits seed releases the Spirit of God, the Angel of your life, to guide you on that path and bring you into that place of God's blessing and anointing. Hallelujah!

First Fruits and Joshua

As I first walked through this study, I uncovered an aspect of God's provision that literally blew me away. In His infinite wisdom and understanding of human need, He has illustrated every one of these seven promises given us in Exodus 23 within the context of His written Word. I have explored some of this territory already. I will give you at least one example from God's Word for each of the seven results of the First Fruits seed.

To see God's illustration of blessing number one, we need to study Joshua, son of Nun. Remember that the Passover, the Feast of Unleavened Bread and the *First Fruits Seed Offering* are all the same great festival. We need to begin in Joshua 5:10:

> *And the children of Israel encamped in Gilgal, and kept the passover on the fourteenth day of the month at even in the plains of Jericho.*

I have been to Gilgal. It's just down from Jericho on the banks of the Jordan. There are just ruins there now, but this is the very place where the children of Israel encamped when they first came into the Promised Land. They had seen the hand of God work on their behalf as they crossed the Jordan River. Joshua had carefully followed all that God instructed him to do and the people had obeyed Joshua as their God-ordained leader.

They had crossed over the Jordan in the first month of the year—a new year, a new land, a new start for the children of Israel. They knew about the three feasts God had commanded them to observe.

While they were camped in Gilgal, they celebrated Passover, the Feast of Unleavened Bread and the *First Fruits Seed Offering.* The children of Israel, under Joshua's guidance, sowed a *First Fruits Seed Offering* because they knew they were coming into a new dimension in their lives.

They could see that they were entering a new place in God. They understood that by giving their First Fruits, they were saying, "God, You are our Partner. God, everything we own belongs to You. God, this is Your undertaking that we are commencing upon now. So, here is our seed. We need You to bless us with a harvest."

The Angel to Meet Their Need

Now their harvest was not going to be wheat at this point in their journey. The all knew they had many battles before them; in fact, Jericho was looming on the horizon directly in front of them. They needed God's blessing and His help as they moved in to take possession of their new land.

Look what happens as a result of their obedience in Joshua 5:13-14:

> *And it came to pass, when Joshua was by Jericho, that he lifted his eyes and looked, and behold, a Man stood opposite him with His sword drawn in His hand. And Joshua went to Him and said to Him, "Are You for us or for our adversaries?" So He said, "No, but as Commander of the army of the Lord I have now come." And Joshua fell on his face to the earth and worshiped, and said to Him, "What does my Lord say to His servant?"*

God was true to His promise. The children of Israel sowed the seed and God released the Angel. That Angel was the captain of the whole army of the kingdom of heaven. Joshua and the children of Israel were facing major military battles. God sent them the Captain of His army to guide them, give them strategies and insure they received their blessing.

You are going to witness six more examples in which the resulting blessings are met by God's releasing an angel and making sure His Word of Exodus 23.

> *For He shall give His angels charge over you, To keep you in all your ways.*
>
> Psalm 91:11

Do you want that result, that blessing, in your own life? Then I am here to show you the principle and reveal the pattern you need to follow to make this a reality in your life today. Only by getting back to this First Fruits Seed Offering can a child of God experience the blessings of the Father in a new and marvelous way. We have only just begun our journey; it's time to move on to the second result of the First Fruits seed offering.

Your Journal Entry:

As we journey, I will make suggestions for entries to your journal. You will need to record highlights of your study, but I will point out points of interest along the way as well. Be open to anything the Holy Spirit may reveal. Make note of these as you will need to refer to them when we complete our journey and prepare to apply all that we have learned.

My suggestion for this chapter is to set aside a page separate from your own notes. Title this page, **"God's Benefit Package."** You are going to witness a full disclosure of the benefits available through your agreement with this Business Partner. God has already anticipated what you will need to succeed. He has given you His written promise and even documented it with testimonies from others who have partnered with Him in the past. We will most likely have one of these pages at the end of each chapter.

So, under **God's Benefit Package,** write:

God says if you will faithfully sow **the First Fruits seed, I will:**

Benefit Number 1: *"send an Angel before you*

    a) *to keep you in the way and*

    b) *to bring you into the place which I have prepared"* (Exodus 23:20).

    c) As your Senior Partner, God adds:

      "Pay attention to him and listen to what he says" (Exodus 23:21, NIV).

    d) Testimonial: Joshua 5:13-14

    e) Personal highlight:

CHAPTER 3

AN ENEMY TO YOUR ENEMIES

"I will be an enemy to your enemies and an adversary to your adversaries. For My Angel will go before you and bring you in to the Amorites and the Hittites and the Perizzites and the Canaanites and the Hivites and the Jebusites; and I will cut them off. You shall not bow down to their gods, nor serve them, nor do according to their works; but you shall utterly overthrow them and completely break down their sacred pillars."

Exodus 23:22-24

Your Business Partner has added considerably to the benefit package in these few verses.

- *"I will be an enemy to your enemies."*
  "I will be an adversary to your adversaries."
  "My Angel will go before you and bring you in." "I will cut them off"—*all* of the "ites" in your life. *"You will utterly overthrow them."*

We have here the most inclusive listing of the enemies of Israel in the Bible. Not one of the various "ites" facing them in the Promised Land has been omitted or overlooked by God. Undoubtedly, the most exciting thing about this benefit is that God says He will be an enemy to their enemies and an adversary to their adversaries. How could one possibly lose under those circumstances?

Look even more closely. It seems this portion of the benefit package has an added feature that is often missed the first time one reads it. We all like the fact that God will be an enemy to our enemies and an adversary to our adversaries. Realize though, what the next part is indicating to the "you" in the promise. What is God's strategy for conquering your enemies and your adversaries?

His Angel *will go before you AND bring you* straight into them, right up to every single one of those "ites" living in **your** Promised Land. Oh, now that can't be right can it? Our natural tendency would be to pray, "Oh God, lead me in a path away from my enemies."

But it says here that the Angel of the Lord will lead you face to face with your enemies, and He doesn't leave a single one out. God has you face all of them.

Now the Bible does go on to say, "and **I will** cut them off." The Hebrew also reads, **"I will** mow them down. **I** will break them away. I will make them turn you loose." Apparently though, we each have to go in, identify and face each one of these enemies and adversaries and then God will deal with them. Then He promises He will cut them off and make them turn you loose.

What kind of "ites" do you need to face? Have you been asking God to keep you away from them? God told His people they had to go in and destroy all the "ites." Why? Only by annihilating them could they be prevented from reproducing.

The Holy Spirit goes before you,
    helps you to identify all your enemies,
        enables you to face each adversary,
            and then God cuts them off.

All the "ites" are accounted for and must be faced. The *pride* of the Amorites, the *religious and moral perversions* of the Canaanites, the *terrorist* Hittites, the *bullying* and *overbearing* Jebusites, the *lack of restraint* associated with the Perizites and the *oppression* of the Hivites all need to be dealt with face-to-face. Your Business Partner promises that He will make them turn you loose.

Then God says **you** will have to completely obliterate every "ite" trying to inhabit your Promised Land. You are **not** to bow down or become a servant to any of them. You are to **overthrow** *their gods, not serve them, nor do according to their works.* You no longer need to be a slave to ungodly habits, evil lusts and other fleshly temptations. God will send His angel to guard you and guide you through each battle. He will target your true enemies and stand with as you fight your way to victory. Paul identifies these real enemies in Ephesians 6:12:

> *We do not wrestle against flesh and blood, but against principalities, against powers, against the rulers of the darkness of this age, against spiritual hosts of wickedness in the heavenly places.*

God promises to declare war on those demon spirits that bring poverty, sickness and lusts into our lives. If God is for us who or what can stand against us (Rom. 8:31)?

GOD PROMISES TO FIGHT THESE ENEMIES AND ADVERSARIES WITH YOU AND TO CUT THEM OFF FOR YOU!

In faith, sow the First Fruits seed. Declare that God is the Owner and you are the partner, albeit the junior partner. And then God will declare war on your enemies. Joshua proves this principle works no matter what sort of enemy you will face.

Victory at Jericho

Then the Lord said to Joshua, "See, I have delivered Jericho into your hands." We need to return to the story of Joshua and the Israelites as they came face-to-face with their enemies at Jericho. Remember, we learned that after they crossed the Jordan River, they celebrated the Passover feast including the **First Fruits Seed Offering.** The Angel, the captain of the Lord's army, spoke to Joshua outside the camp at Gilgal. Because Joshua needed a strategy to defeat their enemies at Jericho, he asked the Angel, "What does my Lord say to His servant?"

Joshua understood this principle and knew Who it was that would ultimately defeat the enemy and bring about victory to the Israelites.

As we begin Joshua 6, we see the situation at Jericho and the answer God sent:

> *Now Jericho was securely shut up because of the children of Israel; none went out, and none came in.*

Jericho appeared impregnable in the natural, but Joshua knew Who was in charge.

30

*And the Lord said to Joshua: "See! **I** have given Jericho into your hand, its king, and the mighty men of valor:"*

Through verse 5 in Joshua 6, the Captain of the Lord's army had given Joshua specific instructions for defeating the enemy at Jericho. God gave them the plan but Joshua and his people had to go in and execute the play. The chapter ends with this confirmation of the blessing resulting from obeying God's commands. Joshua 6:27 reads:

So the Lord was with Joshua, and his fame spread throughout all the country.

Your Journal Entry:

Wouldn't you like to personalize this scripture? Wouldn't you like your name to be there in place of Joshua's? Then you have to follow the same pattern Joshua did. You have to be faithful to observe the feasts, sow the ***First Fruits Seed Offering*** and then follow God's battle plans even when they might seem "odd" to you. Study carefully what God told Joshua and his people to do, the unique strategy He mapped out for them. See what the outcome of their obedience turned out to be. Then get ready to move on in your discovery of God's benefits, the results of adhering to God's way instead of what seems right to man.

Proverbs 14:12 reminds us:

There is a way that seems right to a man, But its end is the way of death.

And Isaiah 55:8-9 states:

"For My thoughts are not your thoughts, Nor are your ways My ways," says the Lord. "For as the heavens are higher than the earth, So are My ways higher than your ways, And My thoughts than your thoughts"

Your Heavenly Business Partner has an advantage over you, His junior partner. He can see not only the beginning but also the ending; in addition He is one hundred percent for your success.

Add these new benefits to **God's Benefit Package:**

God says if you will faithfully sow the First Fruits seed:

Benefit Number 2:

- *"I will be an enemy to your enemies."*
- *"I will be an adversary to your adversaries."*
- *"My Angel will go before you and bring you in."*
- *"I will cut them off"—all* of the "ites" in your life.
- *"You will (be able to) utterly overthrow them."*

Testimonial: Joshua Chapter 6

Record what your part of this deal is to be:

CHAPTER 4

TURN YOUR LITTLE INTO MUCH

"I will bless your bread and water"
Exodus 23:25

There are still more blessings for you to uncover concerning God's Benefit Package. The third result available to you is found in Exodus 23:25.

So you shall serve the Lord your God, and He will bless your bread and your water.

When you read that God is going to bless your bread and water, what comes to your mind' Perhaps it brings to mind what man needs to live, his sustenance. But this speaks of more than just the basics of bread and water that you need for daily existence; it also implies prosperity. By **blessing** these two essentials of life, God can turn your little into much, your poverty into plenty and actually bring about a multiplication to the point at which you are even able to bless others.

Our journey to view the "bread and water" blessing takes us to 1 Kings 17 during the reign of the evil King Ahab. We need to go back a little in time and look at the events leading up to this illustration. God had sent Elijah the prophet to tell King Ahab that there would be neither dew nor rain in the land for the next few years. Then the Lord provided for Elijah by the brook, Cherith. When the brook dried up due to the lack of rain, God sent Elijah to Zarephath. We will pick up our story in 1 Kings 17:8-10:

> *Then the word of the Lord came to him, saying, "Arise, go to Zarephath, which belongs to Sidon, and dwell there. See, I have commanded a widow there to provide for you." So he arose and went to Zarephath. And when he came to the gate of the city, indeed a widow was there gathering sticks. And he called to her and said, "Please bring me a little water in a cup, that I may drink."*

We can perceive from this passage that Elijah knew who to look for and a widow knew he was coming. The Lord had obviously set the stage for His blessing to flow. The right widow woman would know God had sent him and would be ready to be his provision.

So Elijah asked the first widow woman he encountered in Zarephath for a cup of water. If she responded positively, he would know she was the one. God always has our provision in place before we need it. We just need to figure out how to release it.

But I *only have* a handful of flour and a little oil...

Now, I have to admit that I used to read this next part rather carnally. I did not like Elijah's approach to this at all. I had a very low opinion of Elijah's people skills during this exchange with this poor widow. God had to unveil a very significant detail for me so **I** could discern what was really taking place here.

Elijah walked up to the widow woman and said, "Go get me some water, lady." He knew that if she was the one, she would already know that she was to be his provision. So, when she immediately turned to do what he asked, this confirmed she was the right widow. Elijah was on a roll here. A drink of water was nice but God said she was his provision which meant bread **and** water as far as he was concerned. So when the widow turned to go get the water, he spoke over her shoulder. "While you are at it, just get me something to eat, too." How would you have responded to someone like that? Maybe something like, "Now, listen here, prophet. I'll get you some water but **I** don't have a cake— not even a *matzo.*"

As you read these next few verses, see if you can discover what God pointed out to me about His plan and Elijah's part in it:

> *And as she was going to get it, he called to her and said, "Please bring me a morsel of bread in your hand." So she said, "As the Lord your God lives, I do not have bread, only a handful off lour in a bin, and a little oil in a jar; and see, I am gathering a couple of sticks that I may go in and prepare it for myself and my son, that we may eat it, and die."*
>
> 1 Kings 17:11-12

The widow was explaining, making sure this man of God knew about her pathetic situation. She knew he was a man of God, and she understood she was to be his provision, but he needed to know just how bad life had treated her and her son.

Just Give God the Precious

And what did this prophet say in answer to this poor widow's dire circumstances? His answer really upset me. Elijah said, "Don't worry, lady. Go and do what you have said, but make me a cake first."

Do you see that? Now, that used to make me really angry. What I didn't realize is that Elijah also knew he was to be her provision. Elijah wasn't trying to **get** something **from** her; he was trying to **give** something **to** her. He wasn't trying to leach her last dollar; he was trying to get her to give God the precious so that God could give her the everlasting.

Elijah did tell her, "Bring me a cake first." But if we read Elijah's entire reply we come to understand that she was to give her First Fruits offering so God could bless her. Oh, it wasn't timely as far as the calendar was concerned. It wasn't Passover or time for the Feast of Unleavened Bread. It was out of sequence in that respect, but it was the same spirit, the same principle of blessing and increase. Now read all of what Elijah said.

> *And Elijah said to her **"Do not fear; go and do** as you have said, but make me a small cake from it **first**, and bring it to **me;** and **afterward** make some for **yourself** and your son. **For thus says the Lord God of Israel:** The bin of flour shall not be used up, nor shall the jar of oil run dry, until the day the Lord sends rain on the earth.' "*
>
> 1 Kings 17:13-14, **emphasis** added

God is so good. He took the time to explain His resulting blessing to her so that her faith could activate. First God told her not to be afraid. Then He gave her specific instructions on what she was to do. If she would obey God exactly as she was instructed, the blessing would follow. Even though God said there would be provision, she had to give her first fruits before she even fed herself and her son.

There was a definite sequence of events that had to be completed before the blessing could flow. Put yourself in her place. How would you have responded to the prophet's demands? How did the widow respond to Elijah's request?
1 Kings 17:15-16 (NKJV) reports,

> *So she **went** away **and did** according to the word of Elijah,. and she and he and her household ate for many days. The bin off lour was not used up, nor did the jar of oil run dry, according to the word of the Lord which He spoke by Elijah.*

We know that Elijah was a man of God, but this little widow woman shows what she is made of as well. She went and did according to the word of Elijah. She did exactly what he had told her to do. AND THEN they were **all** provided for. She had provision for herself and her son, and she could bless the prophet of God as well. Everything happened
according to the word of the Lord which He spoke to Elijah.

Now, we can do the same thing today. No matter how dire our situation, no matter what the season of the year, our timing may not be right on the calendar timeline, but we can catch up just like this little widow woman did. What did she do? How did she sow to receive the blessing even though it was not the Passover season on the calendar timeline?

She made Elijah a cake first, even before she fed her son or herself. When she sowed the precious into the prophetic, the Bible says then the cruse of oil never failed. The widow had enough oil and enough cakes that, while all the rest of the nation floundered in poverty and drought, she and her family ate aplenty until God changed His method of supply.

The blessing of God was released through her obedience to His instructions.

If you want this kind of blessing to flow in your life, then in the name of the Lord, learn the principle of the *First Fruits Seed Offering.*

- Believe the promise.

- Obey God's instructions.

- Receive the resulting blessing.

- Use your blessing to bless others.

Your Journal Entry:

Think on this before we move on to the next blessing. The instructions given to the widow by Elijah seemed illogical even bordering on irresponsible. This widowed mother had an important decision to make concerning whether she would believe and obey what the Prophet was telling her. As a result of her obedience, she not only received this third blessing but the next one as well.

Time to add to **God's Benefit Package:**

God says if you will faithfully sow the First Fruits Seed Offering:

Benefit Number 3:　**"I** *will bless your bread and water:"* Exodus 23:25

38

By blessing these **two** essentials of life:

- God can turn your little into much,
- transform your poverty into plenty,
- bring about a multiplication in your life, and
- empower you to bless others.

Testimonial: 1 Kings 17:1-16

Personal Highlights:

CHAPTER 5

I WILL TAKE SICKNESS AWAY

"I will take sickness away from the midst of you."
Exodus 23:25b

What a promise! How often have you needed this particular blessing of the Lord? Where is this principle exemplified in the Bible? We will now travel to another time in biblical history, but first I want to finish the story of the widow woman from 1 Kings 17 starting at verse 17.

Now it happened after these things that the son of the woman who owned the house became sick. And his sickness was so serious that there was no breath left in him.

Now the verse just before this one related the blessing that flowed regarding the promise in Exodus 23:25a, the multiplication of the bread and water. Now the widow needs the promise in 23:25b for her son. Elijah is still staying with her and her son in Zarephath. Remember that God had told him to dwell with her. She had already witnessed God move to make provision for them all in spite of the famine and drought all around them. So she confronts Elijah with the condition of her son. He takes the boy and cries out to the

Lord on behalf of the widow. The widow had obeyed God's commands; she had given her first fruits offering and had already received the blessing of bread and water.

Now we read the rest of the story in verses 22-23:

> *Then the Lord heard the voice of Elijah; and the soul of the child came back to him, and he revived. And Elijah took the child and brought him down from the upper room into the house, and gave him to his mother. And Elijah said, "See, your son lives!"*

Although we never learn the name of this widow woman, her obedience in the face of extenuating circumstances is recorded as a powerful testimony of God's faithfulness to His promises when we sow the **First Fruits Seed Offering.**

King Hezekiah Keeps God's Timeline

We are going to explore another illustration of this blessing as well. Travel ahead with me to 2 Chronicles Chapter 29. A new king has just ascended to the throne in Jerusalem. Hezekiah was only twenty-five years old when he became king. The Bible says he did right in the eyes of the Lord as his father David had done. We need to look at the calendar as Hezekiah begins his twenty-nine-year reign.

> *In the first year of his reign, in the first month, he opened the doors of the house of the Lord and repaired them.*
>
> 2 Chronicles 29:3

Remember what we have been learning about God's blessing timeline? God said to work the first month of the year and then do what? Hezekiah had determined to do right in the eyes of the Lord. When he learned about God's timeline he moved to obey it.

> *And Hezekiah sent to all Israel and Judah, and also wrote letters to Ephraim and Manasseh, that they should come to the house of the Lord at Jerusalem, to keep the **Passover** to the Lord God of Israel.*
>
> 2 Chronicles 30:1

Bear in mind that the Passover included the day of Passover, the Feast of Unleavened Bread and the ***First Fruits Seed Offering.*** At Hezekiah's command, couriers went throughout all the land proclaiming it was time for them to return to the Lord, the God of Abraham, Isaac and Israel! Hezekiah wanted to begin his reign by following the instructions of the Lord concerning the feasts passed down to him by King David.

Realize that no feast had been observed in Israel for years and years because of Jezebel and Ahaz. Along came young Hezekiah, the grandson of Ahab and the son of Ahaz, seeking God's heart for the people. This new king tore down the high places of demon worship throughout Israel until they were all utterly destroyed. He also reconstituted the altars of God and re-established the God-ordained feasts throughout the land.

The People Respond to Hezekiah's Decree

Second Chronicles 30:13, 15 records the response of the people of Israel.

> *Now many people, a very great assembly, gathered at Jerusalem to keep the Feast of*

*Unleavened Bread in the second month. Then
they slaughtered the Passover lambs on the fourteenth day of the second month.*

Do you see what they were doing? Read on in 2 Chronicles
30:21:

*So the children of Israel who were present at
Jerusalem kept the Feast of Unleavened Bread
seven days with great gladness.*

We need to look at one more scripture to complete this
renewal of the first feast of the year as commanded by God.

*As soon as the commandment was circulated, the
children of Israel brought in abundance the firstfruits of grain and wine, oil and honey, and of all
the produce of the field; and they brought in
abundantly the tithe of everything.*

2 Chronicles 31:5

The Lord Sent an Angel

We have established the foundation of King Hezekiah's
reign. Journey ahead to 2 Chronicles 32 which records that the
king of Assyria came into Judah to fight against
Jerusalem. King Hezekiah did all he could to prepare his
people for war. Then in 2 Chronicles 32:20-22 we find out
how God blessed Israel as a result of their king's reinstating
these feasts.

*Now because of this King Hezekiah and the
prophet Isaiah, the son of Amoz, prayed and
cried out to heaven. Then the Lord sent an angel
who cut down every mighty man of valor, leader, and
captain in the camp of the king of Assyria. So*

44

> *he returned shamefaced to his own land* ....
> *Thus the Lord saved Hezekiah and the inhabi-*
> *tants of Jerusalem from the hand of Sennacherib the*
> *king of Assyria, and from the hand of all oth-*
> *ers, and guided them on every side* (emphasis
> added).

Again we see the consistency of God's Word as we witness His angel taking care of Hezekiah's enemies and guiding his army on every side. But this godly king had need of the fourth result of the *First Fruits Seed Offering* as we read in 2 Chronicles 32:24:

> *In those days Hezekiah was sick and near death, and*
> *he prayed to the Lord; and He spoke to him and*
> *gave him a sign.*

To complete our story we have to consult with the Prophet Isaiah. He recorded something that is not found here in Chronicles. Read Isaiah 38:1:

> *In those days Hezekiah was sick and near death.*
> *And Isaiah the prophet, the son of Amoz, went to him*
> *and said to him, "Thus says the Lord: 'Set your*
> *house in order, for you shall die and not live.' "*

Don't you just love prophets like that? In comes Isaiah, the man of God. He looks over at the dying king and says, "Well, Hezzie, old buddy, it's over. This is too big. Get your house in order. You are going to die." And then he just walks away. How do you think King Hezekiah, a man whose heart was to serve God, reacted to that word from Isaiah? Look at the next verse. "Hezekiah turned his face to the wall and prayed unto the Lord" (Isaiah 38:2).

"Oh God, I Don't Want to Die!"

What had Hezekiah been doing a few verses before? He had just sowed the *First Fruits Seed Offering.* He had been attempting to follow all of God's previous instructions to the children of Israel. He had seen the angel of the Lord guide them into victory against the foreign enemies. Then he heard Isaiah's message and turned his face to the wall praying, "Oh God, I don't want to die." And the Bible says that he "wept sore." Don't stop here!

Scripture proceeds to say that it came to pass, before Isaiah had come out into the middle court, the word of the Lord came to him. Now I need to stop and draw you a word picture. In those ancient, near eastern houses and palaces, they had an inner bedroom, and then there was a court outside where the family could all gather.

Hezekiah was in that inner bedroom, and before Isaiah could get passed that inner court, the word of the Lord came to him. You see the angel that had been released by Hezekiah's *First Fruits Seed Offering* was still on hand, watching at his post on the wall. So as Isaiah walked out of Hezekiah's room, God instructed the angel to stop him and sent him back in to the praying, weeping king with a revised message.

> *Go and tell Hezekiah, "Thus says the Lord, the God of David your father: 'I have heard your prayer, I have seen your tears; surely I will add to your days fifteen years."*

> Isaiah 38:4-5

Praise God! Hezekiah had released the First Fruits seed blessing, and now the angel was on hand to meet this need as well. God not only took away Hezekiah's sickness, but He also added fifteen years to his life—all because he understood the First Fruits principle! Do you need an angel on hand in your life?

Your Journal Entry:

You should be rejoicing right now. This has been quite a journey so far, wouldn't you agree? We are only at our fourth blessing resulting from sowing a **First Fruits Seed Offering** and we have already witnessed some amazing illustrations of God's "Benefit Package." A widow woman received back her son and King Hezekiah is not only healed but fifteen years was added to his life span. This extended life span leads us right into our next benefit. Believe it or not the blessings just keep getting better and better. God has got us covered every step of the way if we will just be obedient to His instructions.

Add to **God's Benefit Package:**

Benefit Number 4: "1 *will take sickness away from the midst of you."* Exodus 23:25b

Illustrations in:

- 1 Kings 17:17-23—the widow's son

- 2 Chronicles 29:3-33:24 and Isaiah 38:1-5—King Hezekiah

Personal Highlights:

CHAPTER 6

I WILL GIVE You A FULL LIFE SPAN

"The number of thy days I will fulfill."
Exodus 23:26

Exodus 23:26 gives us the fifth result of the First Fruit offering. God says, "And none of you will miscarry and none will be barren in your land. I will give you a full life span" (NIV). What does it mean to have your days fulfilled and have a full life span?

In order to better comprehend what God is giving us here, we are going to study what the word *land* means in the original text. There are two words for *land* in the Bible, *ereth* and *adammah*. The Hebrew word *ereth* is the land of Israel and also represents the earth.

Now, *adammah* is a more interesting and specific word. It refers to the place of an *adam*. An *adam* is an anointed man not an *ish* or an *ohm* or a *lome* or any of those other possible words that could be used for man An *adam* is one that God has His hands on. So an *adammah* is this anointed man's tilled ground. It is where God has called him to function and produce. Since it is his destiny, it includes his family, his job and his ministry.

Adammah is this anointed man's place to labor in the things of God. Did something just jump in your spirit? You need to discern the full impact of what this means to you personally!

The Bible says, "You will not be barren, nor will you miscarry as you operate in your life and ministry under the anointing of God." In other words, you will be fruitful in your labor because God's hand is on you. When you sow your **First Fruits Seed Offering,** it releases an angel that will help you in your decision-making in every area of your life. The angel of God will guide you in your business affairs. The angel of God will come, and, if you will allow him, he will take over the battle in those difficult deals. This angel is there to protect you every step of the way and to keep you on the right path.

Remember that the angel is watching so that he will see the opportunities ahead. He is to guide you to the place God has prepared for you so you will prosper and fulfill the abundant, overflowing future that God has for you.

I have a personal example of how this principle has worked and is working in my own life. I recently built a radio station. I didn't know how I was going to do it, but the Lord showed me His plan. Now the whole city of Columbus is talking about the only local Christian radio station broadcasting within a fifty-mile radius!

Now I have also secured a local TV station that has been in the devil's hands long enough. Because all the cable companies in the area have to carry it, everybody in the town has access to it. God told me He was going to give me that TV station some time ago and now it's a reality!

Before I secured the TV station, I thought I had the deal all wrapped up. I felt I had used the strategies God had given me, but then it seemed as if the enemy moved in and just snatched it away. Now, I want you to see how this principle works in real life situations. The other day I received an interesting call. "Guess what?" the caller said. "The offer that came in three times the offer you made... Well, they have pulled out. They told us they weren't interested at any price. So, now you are number one on the table!"

I had done nothing more on this since they notified me I was out of the picture. So what happened? The angel God sent to watch, guard and guide me, went in and fought the battle for me. I had done all that I was supposed to do. I offered what I was supposed to offer even though another came in much higher than me. God had it covered!

What's true for me is true for you as well. Be faithful to sow the ***First Fruits Seed Offering*** and nothing you do will mis-carry. You will not be barren as you labor in the vineyard to your God.

James and Peter Live Out This Principle

We need to move ahead to the New Testament for our Biblical illustration of this principle. God has promised in Exodus 23:26, **"I** will give you a full lifespan."

We need to get ahold of the full extent of this exciting rev-elation. The result will be that we will live not only better but also longer.

Let's visit the early first-century church in Jerusalem. Acts 12 starts out with King Herod's arresting some followers of Christ just to vex (irritate, annoy, torment) the church. I used to wonder about what happened here, so I asked God,

"How come we lost James but not Peter?" Carefully read Acts 12:1-3 to see if you can discover what God revealed to me based on what you have learned so far in this study.

> *Now about that time Herod the king stretched forth his hands to vex certain of the church. And he killed James the brother of John with the sword. And because he saw it pleased the Jews, he proceeded further to take Peter also. (Then were the days of unleavened bread.)*

What was the church doing at this time? They were in the midst of celebrating the Feast of Unleavened Bread. From the sequence of events, we can figure that they have already celebrated Passover and are near the end of the week-long feast. About the time Herod arrested James, they were preparing for the ***First Fruits Seed Offering.***

Now, Herod had arrested James before the Christians got their seed into the ground. But then he arrested Peter and kept him in prison. As the church was praying without ceasing, they completed the feast and got the seed in the ground. Look at Acts 12:4:

> *So when he had arrested him, he put him in prison, and delivered him to four squads of soldiers to keep him, intending to bring him before the people after Passover (emphasis added).*

That means Herod intended to kill Peter but not until after Passover. The church at Jerusalem kept the Passover, the Feast of Unleavened Bread, and then they planted the First Fruits offering. What has to happen when the First Fruits seed is given?

> *And when Herod would have brought Peter forth, the same night Peter was sleeping between two*

*soldiers, bound with two chains. And the keepers before the door kept the prison, and behold, the angel **of the Lord came upon him** ....*

The angel came upon Peter, released him from his chains and guided him safely out of the prison. The Bible says that the angel came up, slapped Peter on the side and said, "Get up! This is not your time to die." Peter had to fulfill his days! Hallelujah! We know from Scripture that Peter did indeed have a lot more to do before his lifespan was completed. Read First and Second Peter for further insight into his mission on earth.

The same principle applies in your life. The First Fruits seed releases the angel of God to meet you, lengthen your life and fulfill His purpose. God promises a full life in both quality and quantity! This is exciting news but there is even more to our benefits package. God, our Business Partner, wants us to be more than just healthy and live a long life. He wants us to increase and possess the land! We have two more results yet to go.

Your Journal Entry:

This has been another exciting chapter revealing even more of how God desires to bless His children when they obey His instructions. There are times when we are not even aware of the far-reaching effects sowing our **First Fruits Seed Offering** can bring. In spite of the persecution by

Herod, the early church remained faithful to keep the Passover. We know they sowed in prayer and we saw the amazing results in the rescue of Peter right out from under the noses of Herod's guards. Is any situation too difficult for the God we serve?

Add to **God's Benefit Package:**

Benefit number 5: *"I will give you a full life span."* (Exodus 23:26)

    a) You will not miscarry or be barren in your land.

    b) Your labor in your adammah will be fruitful

    c) Peter's Testimony in Acts 12:4-11.

Personal Highlights:

CHAPTER 7

You WILL INCREASE AND INHERIT

"You will be increased and inherit the land."
Exodus 23:30

God is the head and not the tail. I, therefore, am the head and not the tail. I will be increased and not decrease. I will grow and not be diminished, and so will you. You need to take a moment and read the following scripture passage out loud replacing the words "you or yours" with your name to get this powerful promise from God into your spirit.

"The Lord will open to you His good treasure, the heavens, to give the rain to your land in its season, and to bless all the work of your hand. You shall lend to many nations, but you shall not borrow. And the Lord will make you the head and not the tail; you shall be above only, and not be beneath, if you heed the commandments of the Lord your God, which I command you today, and are careful to observe them."
Deuteronomy 28:12-13

You will enter your *adammah,* your land, your destiny, your place in God. You will come to understand and know who you are in God and what your purpose is on this planet. Sounds pretty amazing, doesn't it? Well, it's true!

Think back to the beginning of our journey. We looked at a great warrior and leader named Joshua. We saw how the Angel came to him after he and the children of Israel celebrated the Passover, the Feast of Unleavened Bread and sowed the First Fruits Seed Offering. You need to read the whole story of Joshua and the many conquests he led God's people through in the land God had promised to them even before they crossed the Jordan River. Joshua declared he would serve the Lord and his life testified that he did.

God had a plan, a divine purpose for Joshua and the children of Israel. He had a destiny for Joshua to fulfill. Go back for a minute to the beginning of the story, before they entered the Promised Land. Carefully study this important piece of history to receive the insight you will need to prosper in our own Promised Land.

> *After the death of Moses the servant of the Lord, it came to pass that the Lord spoke to Joshua the son of Nun, Moses' assistant, saying: "Moses My servant is dead. **Now** therefore, **arise, go** over this Jordan, you and all this people, to the **land** which **I** am **giving** to them—the children of Israel."*
> Joshua 1:1-2, **emphasis** added

God told them it was time for them to arise, go and enter the land He was giving them. They needed to cross over the Jordan and physically enter their Promised Land. Carefully watch for vital clues for activating this principle in your life. God gets even more specific in His instructions and the extent of His promises.

"Every place that the sole of your foot will tread upon I have given you, as I said to Moses. From the wilderness and this Lebanon as far as the great river, the River Euphrates, all the land of the Hittites, and to the Great Sea toward the going down of the sun, shall be your territory. No man shall be able to stand before you all the days of your life; as I was with Moses, so I will be with you. I will not leave you nor forsake you. Be strong and of good courage, for to this people you shall divide as an inheritance the land which I swore to their fathers to give them."

Joshua 1:3-5, **emphasis** added

I **will not leave you nor forsake you.** Read that again. The NIV translation reads, **"I** will **never** leave you nor forsake you." You may have read this portion of scripture many times, but look at it with fresh vision. Never forsaking you means God will never abandon or leave you in the lurch. If you have ever begun a project that depended on someone else's help to complete it and they didn't follow through, then you know how it feels to be forsaken.

God was revealing Joshua's inheritance and assuring him that He would personally stay with him through the whole process of possessing it. There are some instructions for Joshua in this passage, though, that we must be careful not to overlook. God said He was going to be right there with him every step of the way, but Joshua had some responsibilities within the joint venture as well.

"Every place that the sole of your foot will tread upon **I** have given you." Joshua had to go place his foot on the land in order to inherit it. God had already given it to him but Joshua and the people had to go in and take possession of that Promised Land.

"Be strong and of good courage, for to this people you shall divide as an **inheritance** the land." Joshua had to be strong and courageous, remembering that God was with Him. Then it was his job to divide the land up as an inheritance among the people. That phrase, "Be strong and of good courage" was used several more times in this interchange between God and Joshua. Any time God repeats something, we need to take special notice and pay close attention to what follows that phrase.

> *"Only be strong and very courageous, that you may **observe to do according to all the law** which Moses My servant commanded you; do not turn from it to the right hand or to the left, that you may prosper wherever you go. This Book of the Law shall not depart from your mouth, but you shall meditate in it day and night, that you may **observe to do according to all** that is written in it."*
>
> Joshua 1:7-8a, emphasis added

Joshua's destiny was to be the leader of God's people and make sure they not only knew but also obeyed **all** the Law. As the person in charge, he was to meditate on the Law day and night. God was also warning him that he would need to stand strong in his convictions and not swerve off dead center so that the benefits would be released.

> *For then you will make your way prosperous, and then you will have good success. Have **I** not commanded you? Be strong and of good courage; do not be afraid, nor be dismayed, for the Lord your God is with you wherever you go."*
>
> Joshua 1:8b-9

One more time God says to Joshua, "Be strong and of good 58

courage; do not be afraid, nor be dismayed, for the Lord your God is with **you wherever you** go." It is interesting to note here that God said He would be with Joshua wherever Joshua would go. Wherever Joshua put his foot, the land was his. Wherever **he** would go, God would go **with him.** What an awesome existence this implies is available to one who determines to serve and obey the Lord.

Let me make a statement that will amaze you. Are you ready to receive a powerful truth? **God has never wasted a single minute of your life.** That's right! You are far too precious to Him. Now, you may waste a lot of time or dissipate large portions of energy. But God is not going to waste so vital a resource. Every occurrence in your life is *preparation, preservation* or *presentation* to insure fulfillment of His divine purpose for you here on this planet. Consider for a moment what this encompasses. Every wilderness experience, each mountain top encounter or any moment spent in the valley will fall within one of these three categories.

Now let's finish the story of Joshua. Travel ahead with me to the end of Joshua's life. Joshua knows he is about to die after living 110 years! He gathers all of the leaders of his people together to address them one last time. Turn in your Bible to Joshua 23:1-5.

> *Now it came to pass, a long time after the Lord had given rest to Israel from all their enemies round about, that Joshua was old, advanced in age. And Joshua called for all Israel, for their elders, for their heads, for their judges, and for their officers, and said to them: "I am old, advanced in age. You have seen all that the Lord your God has done to all these nations because of you, for the Lord your God is He who has*

God will fight for you. God will expel your enemies before you. God will be your Business Partner. God will be your Finance Partner. God will be your Life Partner. God will be your Physician. You shall possess the land God has promised you. You will even leave an inheritance to those that follow you.

Did you get a chance to see the four great preachers on *Larry King Live?* One of them from San Diego shared about a woman who had come to the church for prayer because she was sick. Larry King spoke up and said, "But that's a crutch." For me, the high spot of the whole program was this preacher's reply: "Larry, Jesus isn't just a crutch to me. He is a whole hospital."

Glory to God! God will become your Partner in life, and if it's about business, then you are going to make a profit. If it's health, you will be whole. Whatever you need to fulfill God's purpose in your life, He will provide it. As a matter of fact, He already has it waiting for you. Read this amazing testimony of Joshua's life in chapter 23:14:

> *"Behold, this day **I** am going the way of all the earth. And you know in all your hearts and in all your souls that not one thing has failed of all the good things which the Lord your God spoke concerning you. **All have come to pass for you; not***

one word of them has failed" (emphasis added).

Joshua declared that not one good thing God had spoken concerning his destiny had failed. How could he say that? Wouldn't you like to be able to say that at the end of your life? What a powerful eulogy to have spoken in your honor. In order to make that statement though, you would have to have known what God had said about you. Isn't that right? You would have to have been confident that you had fol- lowed the path God had predestined for you. You would have to be able to say like Paul did at the end of his life, "I have fought the good fight, **I** have finished the race [that was marked out for me], I have kept the faith" (see 2 Tim. 4:7 and Rom. 12:1).

That leads us right into our final benefit for sowing the **First Fruits Seed Offering.** But take a quick moment and make some important notations in your journal. Then we can complete this study of the seven blessings so you can begin implementing all of them in your own life!

Your Journal Entry:

Make a note to yourself to find out what God has predes- tined for you to complete during your life time. Time to make your calling and election sure! (2 Peter 1:10).

Add to **God's Benefit Package:**

Benefit Number 6: *"You will be increased and inherit the land."* Exodus 23:30

    a) **You** will enter **your** *adammah,* **your** land, **your** destiny, **your** place in God.

    b) **You** will understand and know who **you** are in God

    c) **You** can know what **your** purpose is on this planet.

    d) *"The Lord will open to **you** His good treasure,*

    e) [He will] *bless all the work of **your** hand.*

    f) ***You** shall lend to many nations, but you shall not borrow.*

    g) *The Lord will make **you** the head and not the tail; **you** shall be above only, and not be beneath* (Deuteronomy 28:12-13).

    h) God will never leave you nor forsake you.

    i) God will not waste a moment of your life. You are in *preparation, preservation* or *presentation.*

    j) Testimonial in Joshua chapter 23.

Personal Highlights:

CHAPTER 8

FIRST FRUITS SEED OFFERING RESULT NUMBER 7

RECOVER WHAT THE ENEMY HAS STOLEN

"I will deliver the inhabitants of the land into your hand, and you will drive them out[!]"
                                        Exodus 23:31

God has again given you His promise to make sure you succeed in the destiny He has in place for you. Can you see that He is one hundred percent for your success? He promises to deliver the inhabitants of the land, your land, into your hand. Look again at this verse, though. Now you must also do something to activate the full promise. Do you see it? God will deliver, but you are to then drive those illegal inhabitants out of your land!

The bottom line is you will have to go right into the enemy camp and take back what he has stolen from you. He cannot have your children! They belong to the Lord. He cannot ruin your health! It belongs to the Lord. He cannot take your finances! You are God's business partner, and God says you will make a profit, not suffer loss. The battle has been won; the enemy is a defeated foe. All you have to do is kick him out of your land! Oh, I don't know about you, but I get excited about this revelation!

David. **I** am sure you know the stories of David and know that his heart was to obey and serve God. God shared what He thought about David in Acts 13:22: "I have found David the son of Jesse, a man after My own heart, who will do all My will." We know that David kept the ways of the Lord. All His laws and decrees David followed according to Psalms 18:21-22 and 2 Samuel 22:22-23. Many of the Psalms talk about how God delivered David from the hands of his enemies.

David faced many challenges in his lifetime but one exemplifies our point here. Go with me back to the time when David, though anointed by Samuel as Israel's king, was running from Saul's army. 1 Samuel 30 begins with David and his men returning to Ziklag where they had left their families and possessions while they were off at war. When they got to Ziklag, they found it destroyed by fire and their wives, sons and daughters taken captive. David asked the Lord what he was to do about this.

> *So David inquired of the Lord, saying, "Shall **I** pursue this troop? Shall **I** overtake them?" And He answered him, "Pursue, for you shall surely overtake them and without fail **recover all.**"*
> 1 Samuel 30:8, **emphasis** added

David obeyed God's instructions and he took back all that the enemy had stolen.

> *So David recovered all that the Amalekites had carried away, and David rescued his two wives. And nothing of theirs was lacking, either small or great, sons or daughters, spoil or anything which they had taken from them; **David recovered all.***
> 1 Sam. 30:18-19

The Day the Sun Stood Still

We know from our previous study that Joshua kept the
Passover and faithfully followed the decrees of the Lord
passed down to him by Moses. Joshua chapter 10 gives us an
amazing example of what extraordinary lengths God will go to
in order to insure victory for those who obey His commands.

> *And the Lord said to Joshua, "Do not fear them, for*
> *I have delivered them into your hand; not a man of*
> *them shall stand before you."*
>
> Joshua 10:8

Travel ahead a few verses to Joshua   10:10-14 for the
account of the battle.

> *So the Lord routed them before Israel, killed them with*
> *a great slaughter at Gibeon, chased them along*
> *the road that goes to Beth Horon, and struck*
> *them down as far as Azekah and Makkedah.*
> *And it happened, as they fled before Israel and were*
> *on the descent of Beth Horon, that the Lord cast*
> *down large hailstones from heaven on them as far*
> *as Azekah, and they died. There were more who*
> *died from the hailstones than the children of Israel*
> *killed with the sword. Then Joshua spoke to the Lord*
> *in the day when the Lord delivered up the*
> *Amorites before the children of Israel, and he*
> *said in the sight of Israel: "Sun, stand still over*
> *Gibeon; And Moon, in the Valley of Aijalon." So the*
> *sun stood still, And the moon stopped, Till the*
> *people had revenge upon their enemies. Is this not*
> *written in the Book of Jasher? So the sun stood still*
> *in the midst of heaven, and did not hasten to go*
> *down*

You are to drive out your enemies and occupy your land! You are to take back what the enemy has stolen! You are to fulfill your destiny, your divine purpose! God will do whatever it takes to see that your victory is sure!

Your Journal Entry:

This is an exciting time in our study. There have been so many awesome benefits revealed to us by our loving Father, our Business Partner, and our God.

This last revelation, though, should have really ignited your spirit. If you have any family member, child or parent that the enemy has tried to convince you he has captured, you now know he has no legal right to them. As you initiate the process by giving your *First Fruits Seed Offering,* you activate the forces of God to come against your enemies and deliver them into your hands. Your victory is sure as you lock into these principles and begin to walk along God's blessing timeline.

So let's add the seventh resulting blessing to **God's Benefit Package:**

Benefit Number 7: **"I** *will deliver the inhabitants of the land into your hand, and you will drive them out[!]1""* (Exodus 23:31).

a) You can take back what the enemy has stolen from you.

b) You can drive out the illegal inhabitants from your land.

c) God will do whatever it takes to deliver your enemies into your hands.

d) Testimonial: David recovered all in 1 Sam. 30:8, 18, 19; Joshua saw the sun stand still in Joshua 10:8-14.

Personal highlights:

CHAPTER 9

HOW IMPORTANT IS THE FIRST FRUITS OFFERING?

THE GREATEST DEMONSTRATION OF THE POWER

Now, how important is this truth? How central is this principle to the Word of the living God? I have shown you that these results are laced all through the Scriptures. The greatest demonstration of the power of the First Fruit seed though is in Jesus Himself.

God Sowed the Greatest First Fruits Seed

God practiced this vital principle Himself. God sowed the greatest seed of all time on the day of First Fruits following the Passover. In Matthew 26:17, you will see that on the first day of the Feast of Unleavened Bread, the Passover Day, Jesus sent His disciples to go and prepare a room where they then conducted what we generally refer to as the Lord's Supper. Look at what Jesus told His disciples in verse 18:

> *Go into the city to a certain man, and say to him, "The Teacher says, 'My time is at hand; I will keep the Passover at your house with My disciples."*

In Luke 22:15-16, Jesus says to His disciples,

> *"With fervent desire **I** have desired to eat this Passover with you before **I** suffer; for **I** say to you, **I** will no longer eat of it until it is fulfilled in the kingdom of God."*

We have learned that the Feast of Unleavened Bread, or the Passover, always ends with the First Fruits Seed Offering. So, when Jesus went out into the Garden of Gethsemane to pray, He was fully aware of what was coming. He knew that He was to be God's **First Fruit Seed Offering.** But He said, "Father, if there is any way this can pass, let it pass. But nevertheless, not My will but Thine be done." We know the rest of the story. But do we realize that Jesus, God's own Son, was sown into the earth as the **First Fruits Seed Offering?**

1 Corinthians 15:20-23 tells us that Jesus became that First Fruit. Jesus taught this very principle back in John 12:24:

> *"Most assuredly, **I** say to you, unless a grain of wheat falls into the ground and dies, it remains alone; but if it dies, it produces much grain."*

God's Divine Harvest

When the offering is planted in God's name as God's seed, it will flourish forth into the blessings of God. According to God's timeline, what was released fifty days later? Next on God's calendar is Pentecost, the outpouring of the Holy Spirit. Now you and **I** are God's divine harvest from His First Fruits Seed. We need to discover how this pattern applies to each of us so that His seed will multiply through us on the earth.

The entire death and resurrection of Jesus was carried out by God at the Feast of Unleavened Bread!

- Jesus Himself was the **Passover Lamb.**

- **His** last seven days on earth were the Days of **Unleavened** Bread!!

- ON FIRSTFRUITS SUNDAY, HE AROSE FROM THE DEAD AND BECAME THE "FIRST **FRUITS SEED"!**

Remember our lesson on the calendar. Passover always leads to Pentecost. Pentecost brings the outpouring of the Holy Spirit. That leads us to atonement and reconciliation to our God. We have come full circle. We are back to where we started. Our journey started in Exodus 23, led us through several books of the Bible and into the lives of many of its heroes.

You have kept a detailed journal of your journey. You have discovered powerful truths and uncovered life changing principles in God's Word. Now you need to see how to apply what you have learned to bring about breakthrough in your life, your family and your ministry.

Don't neglect to go all the way to the end with this. Do not stop short of walking out this principle in your own life. Don't end your journey without obtaining the treasure, the blessings available to you. Take the time to complete the last chapter and move into that new dimension of God.

Nothing we learn is useful until it can be applied to our lives. Chapter Ten will guide you through to some practical application, some steps to begin the process in your own life.

To stop now, short of entering your Promised Land, would

be foolish. Remember those tribes that chose to stay on the east side of the Jordan when Joshua and the rest of the children of Israel crossed over? Don't stay behind. Possess the land God has prepared for you, your family and those you are called to touch with your ministry!

Your Journal Entry:

Congratulations! You have worked hard and discovered for yourself he awesome blessings of the ***First Fruits Seed Offering.***

Complete this last journal entry and then use your journal along with the steps provided in the next chapter to ignite this power in your own life. God is waiting to shower you with all that the seven blessings can produce in your land.

Add to **God's Benefit Package:**

- Passover always leads to Pentecost.

- Pentecost brings the outpouring of the Holy Spirit.

- The spirit leads us to atonement and reconciliation to our God.

- Now you are God's divine harvest from His First Fruits Seed.

- Jesus Himself was the **Passover Lamb. 72**

- Jesus' last seven days on earth were the Days of **Unleavened** Bread!!

- ON FIRSTFRUITS SUNDAY, JESUS AROSE FROM THE DEAD AND BECAME THE "FIRST FRUITS **SEED**"!

CHAPTER 10

FINAL WORD

How You CAN HAVE THE BENEFITS OF THE FIRST FRUITS SEED OFFERING

In order to step into the benefits of the *First Fruits Seed Offering,* you must have a renewed mind in Christ with this mindset:

1. Be *aware* of its meaning and significance.

   - You now know!

   - The door is open!

2. Realize:

   - "Thou shalt keep the Feast"—It is not optional.

   - "Thou shalt not come before Me empty"—Bring a SEED!

3. **Prepare** and **bring** your seed.

   - It is "the first and best of your **land"** *(adamah—* field of labor, ministry).

   - It determines your harvest for the rest of the year!

   - "He who sows sparingly shall also reap sparingly" (2 Cor. 9:6).

- "Whatsoever a man sows, that shall he also reap" (Gal. 6:7).

4. *Expect* a sevenfold harvest when you sow!

   a. God will release His *"Angel."*

   b. Your enemies will be His *enemies.*

   c. God will *bless* your bread and water.

   d. God will take *sickness* away from you.

   e. God will give you a *full life* in quality and quantity.

   f. God will cause you to *increase* and inherit.

   g. God will drive out all who keep you from your destiny.

5. *Do not delay.* It's not too late to start. Begin by using these steps.

Experience Your Breakthrough Now!

Take these steps for yourself:

1. Look back over the journal you have been keeping throughout this journey. List here specific highlights revealed along the way by the Holy Spirit.

2.   What do you feel the meaning and significance of the
     First Fruit offerings is for you personally?

3. You need to determine what the definition of your
   "land" is. Ask the Lord to reveal clearly what this is for
   you.

4. Review 2 Corinthians 9:6 and Galatians 6:7.

5. Determine what your ***First Fruits Seed Offering*** is to
   be. Set a specific number as you obey the voice of God:
   $

6.   What is the harvest you expecting as a result for this
     year?

7. What enemies do you see that you need to face this
   year?

8. What did you learn about handling your enemies?
   Review results 2, 4, 7.

9. Locate a calendar that gives the dates for this year's Passover, Pentecost and Feast of Tabernacles. Mark those dates on your day planner.

Date for Passover:

Date for Pentecost:

Date for the Feast of Tabernacles:

10. Once you have sown your First Fruits offering, keep a journal of the results you see in your life. Document this for the upcoming year and review it as you begin next year.

11. Reread the full accounts of the examples presented in the lesson we just walked through. Ask the Lord to show you any insights you might need for your journey. Highlight areas that resemble incidents in your own life.

12. Enjoy the blessings of sowing your First Fruits Seed Offering.

I am praying this prayer for you:

In the name of Jesus, I call down blessing and anointing. I declare health; I declare life; I declare strength; I declare financial blessing upon you as you sow your First Fruits seed offering. I declare breakthrough in your life in the name of Jesus . . . a new dimension of life and power in your life as you obey His commands. In Jesus' mighty name, Amen.

ABOUT THE AUTHOR

Dr. Ronald E. Cottle has served as a pastor of churches. He has been president of a university and a seminary and is the author of more than fifty books and fifty Bible college courses. He is the founder of Christian Life School of Theology and Beacon University.

Dr. Cottle has earned an A.B. degree from Florida Southern College, Lakeland, Florida; a Master of Divinity from Lutheran Theological Southern Seminary, Columbia, South Carolina; and a Ph.D. in Religion from the University of Southern California, Los Angeles. He also earned a Master of Science (M.S.Ed.) in Education and an Ed.D. from U.S.C. He also holds the honorary Doctor of Divinity.

See www.roncottle.com for more information and resources from Dr. Cottle.

Dr. Cottle has worked tirelessly in his home office for the past two decades compiling his five hundred notebooks, fifty plus college courses, fifty plus books, hundreds of sermon outlines, publications, articles and newsletters. Dr. Cottle and Dr. Thomas Hale are cataloging everything into an online library.

The library contains digital files (PDF and Microsoft Word) available for download, streaming audio files and streaming video files.

The library is available for a small monthly subscription. Please visit the library at: www.cottlelibrary.com

www.ingramcontent.com/pod-product-compliance
Lightning Source LLC
Chambersburg PA
CBHW052219150726
48002CB00003B/1189